A JOURNAL OF THE Year of the Pharmacy:

BEING

Obſervations or Memorials,

Of the moſt Remarkable

OCCURRENCES,

As well

PUBLIC *as* PRIVATE,

Which happened in

AN ARTIST'S MIND

During the

GREAT VISITATIONS

In 2020.

Written by an ARTIST who continued all the while in *Brooklyn*. Never made public before.

Pablo Helguera

A Journal of the Year of the Pharmacy

Four Express Scripts (and a Preamble)

Jorge Pinto Books
New York

A Journal of the Year of the Pharmacy:
Four Express Scripts (and a Preamble)

Jorge Pinto Books Inc.
3101 New Mexico Av. NW,
Washington DC, 20016
jpinto@mac.com.

ISBN: 978-1-7364215-3-6

Design: Charles King: www.ckmm.com

A Journal of the Year of the Pharmacy premiered at the Tribeca Performing Arts Center, New York, on October 15, 2021, as part of a solo exhibition of the same name at the Shirley Fiterman Art Center curated by Lisa Panzera.

The original cast of the play included

Pablo Helguera (self)

Corey Tasmania (Arizona)

Brian Linden (Steinway)

The production was directed by Sarah Hughes.

Osco

Lights go on the empty stage. Pablo is standing in center stage.

Pablo

I love places that have a history, or a cultural or religious meaning. I love archaeological sites, old churches, obscure museums where I am the only visitor. But drug stores, those with pharmacies in them, play a special role in my life.

Over my adult life I developed a mild obsession with pharmacies. It was not until about a year ago when I finally realized the true reason for that obsession.

But first, let me explain my relationship with those places.

Growing up, the closest pharmacy was around the corner of the house. They had a Pac-Man console, and my brother and I would go there practically every afternoon after school to play. It was one of the first examples of how both he and I could become obsessive about things.

The pharmacy, which had a light green interior with fluorescent lights and glass counters, also had that smell that is distinct to all Mexican pharmacies, a mixture of crushed aspirins, rubbing alcohol, and calamine lotion.

I should say that it is not that I consider drugstores particularly interesting. Instead, I am precisely obsessed with everyday, corporate, superficial looking, commercial, shallow, drugstores.

I love them because they are artless. I love them precisely because they help me escape from art, something I need often. They are a medicine for escapists like me.

I love them because they preach a contrived commercial gospel of wellness, which I know full well is a fairy tale, a children's story. Still, I like their ubiquity, the fact that there is one on every corner and that they all look exactly the same.

The neutral colors of the pharmacy, meant to convey sterility, would foreshadow my future working in art museums, with their brightly lit, neutral white walls. Yet, when I think of pharmacies I am not interested in artists who made art about them like Joseph Cornell or Damien Hirst. I am interested in pharmacies because they are sites that regulate extremes, like between healing and recovery. They are not places built for drama. They are places for supporting our basic biological functions. And often our needs of beauty as well. They are repositories of first aid items but also shaving cream. Of Tylenol and Motrin but also Tres Semmé conditioner; a place to refill a prescription and to get makeup remover.

Pharmacies, the boring commercial kind, underscore the equalizing fact that we all have bodies, rich and poor, smart and not, beautiful and ugly, and we all are going to face the end of life.

Throughout my life, I always enjoyed walking into pharmacies. In Mexico City, I would go into the pharmacy section of Sanborns, the one that was directly across the street from my aunt's office, and I would acquire a glass bottle of red mouthwash, supposedly made after a formula conceived by a French chemist. The bottle looked elegant, and the mouthwash seemed to me like a powerful tonic.

Over the years, and for some reason increasingly over the last 10 years, on my way home from work I would go into a drugstore and buy something or pretend to buy something. Usually it was a small toy for Estela, which I brought home until she got tired of Rite Aid toys. But going into drugstores became a kind of therapy for me.

A year and a half ago, in March 2020, I woke up with a fever. I had lost my sense of smell and taste. As my fever climbed to 103 and I had hallucinatory visions, the nights became visits to the abyss. My head was on fire and my body shivered violently. I dreamt of the Commendatore, the stone statue that arrives in Don Giovanni's lair to take him to hell.

Nearby our house in Brooklyn people started to die by the hundreds per day. I learned of colleagues and neighbors who had been taken away.

Then one morning, the fever broke. I began a long way to recovery. I had been spared this time.

We were all confined in our homes, going to the drug store next to the neighborhood park was our only possible outing. Buying Dove body wash, finding the ever-scarce Bounty paper towels and the even more scarce Lysol cleaner or even Purell became a thrilling experience. We became a hunter/gatherer society in the pursuit of those items. During those early days, the shelves where those products once stood were totally empty.

At some point I realized that the truck that delivered the weekly shipments to the drug store arrived on Tuesday afternoons. So I would walk to the drugstore on those days, like the main character in Gabriel García Márquez's *No One Writes to the Colonel*, a story about a Colonel visiting the post office daily to find out if his pension check has arrived.

On one of those days, as I was waiting in aisle 4 next to the cat food for the drug store attendant to unload a delivery—somewhere between the vitamin section and the bandages—I had an epiphany.

It was one of those insights that are hard to describe in words, and can only be explained through images or by being there.

It is understanding through navigation, through simply walking. Places have languages, and our bodies have a physical/corporeal/spatial understanding. It is through the conjunction of those two that we can understand things that we have not been able to understand before.

I thought of a drug store I remembered from 1989, the year my family emigrated to Chicago. We lived on Campbell Avenue, in Chicago's West Rodgers Park Area, close to Lincoln Avenue, an area full of mysterious budget hotels. New to the American way of life, I often wondered, "why would tourists stay in hotels in our neighborhood?"

My room had a window overlooking a Korean restaurant. The barbecue smell from that restaurant reminded me powerfully of summers in Mexico City and of my friends who I missed so much.

We also had an Osco across the street. My dad liked that there was an ATM at the drugstore, a novelty for us. He said the words "cash station" in an exaggerated English accent, which my mom hated. As recent immigrants, were struggling financially. On special occasions, like birthdays, my dad sometimes bought soaps and shampoo at the store for my mom, thinking they were fine items.

I personally loved the office supply section. I still love the office supply section. I also particularly loved the term "Express Scripts." It made me think that you could purchase plays from the pharmacists.

One Sunday evening in late summer of 1990, I went to Osco with my dad to buy milk. 2% milk. When we were crossing the street I saw the deep blue sky of dusk and the reverse red letters of the Osco pharmacy reflected on his glasses. I associated the blue color with the 70s, and the 70s with my childhood, and with him. And I associated the red light with happy activities.

I knew this everyday trip to Osco was one of those events that would be totally forgettable, something that no one should remember, and I remember thinking that I needed to remember that very moment for that very reason. I had always felt that my role in life was to be a memory preserver, to save moments that had been left unperceived by others, and record/document/memorialize them for posterity. It was precisely the banality of that moment, accompanied by the awareness that I felt that one day, on a day like today, my dad would no longer be around and I would painfully miss him, that made me realize that it was important to save the memory.

Places, memories, blue glass, red letters, milk, office supplies, the 1970s. Eau de toilette, Mexico City, Chicago, budget hotels, Lincoln Avenue, Osco.

This body remembers.

First Aisle

A bathroom materials showroom in Mexico City.

Arizona walks to center stage.

Arizona

I have recently realized that everything I have truly learned in life has been by walking. I have learned it not through my mind, but through my body.

The thing is, I had not realized this until a few days ago, after many years of going to school and reading, of obsessively going deep into the entrails of knowledge.

Not that reading was not important. Reading was only the reason for my walking.

The most important education I had was in the streets.

I don't know if I am a peripatetic artist. I only believe in the significance of distances, in space and time. And I believe that walking is a form of reading.

And I grew up in a place, that, if it were a book, it would probably be a strangely translated novel.

I grew up in a house in Colonia Nápoles, in Mexico City. It is a middle-class neighborhood, full of curious street names. For starters, why did someone decide to call the entire neighborhood "Nápoles," like Naples, Italy? That place has absolutely nothing to do with Naples. Continuing that incongruity, the streets of our neighborhood were named after American cities and states: Oklahoma, Chicago, Indianápolis, Filadelfia. We lived at Arizona ciento seis (106), between Nueva York and, Pensilvania. The pharmacy, by the way, was located on the corner of Pensilvania and Rochester.

I try to envision that time. I am about 15 years old and have finally been allowed to walk around town by myself. At that age I already know I want to become an artist. I feel impatient, worried that I am wasting my time, that I will never accomplish my objectives if I remain where I am. My family has many books, but very few of them are about modern art—the art books are mostly of historical periods.

I am desperate to connect with the present. And I don't know where to go.

So I walk out in search of it.

I walk endlessly through the streets of Rochester, Nebraska, Texas, Idaho.

The closest cultural center near our house is the Polyforum Siqueiros, next to what was then known as el Hotel de México. El hotel de México was supposed to be the largest hotel in the country and perhaps in the world. It seemed to be permanently under construction, as if it had been a metaphor of the modern project of Latin America.

The Polyforum had been commissioned in the 1960s by the owner of the hotel de Mexico to David Alfaro Siqueiros, then the most famous living Mexican artist and the last remaining survivor of the big three Mexican muralists. He would build the largest mural in the world, something larger than the Sistine Chapel.

The mural is indeed the largest, and in addition, perhaps the ugliest, ever made. It is a mass of black metal with grotesque masses of people, entitled "La marcha de la humanidad en la tierra y hacia el cosmos." It is a kind of narrative of the birth of humanity and its cultural progression from myth and ritual to some kind of social utopia after overcoming tyranny and oppression.

Like the Hotel de Mexico, the mural also seemed somehow unfinished, in particular a huge black metal fence in the background of the painting that seemed under construction.

Especially interesting to me was the Polyforum's exhibition space, which only had a single, sleepy attendant at the counter. I went to that bookstore a million times. I must have been the only customer who ever went in.

I purchased a number of books about Mexican art, including Diego Rivera's diaries, Siqueiros' own artistic manifesto "No hay más ruta que la nuestra" ("there is no other road than ours") and his book on how to paint a mural (which was of course what I wanted to do). I read feverishly, devouring books about the history of Mexico City, which I was in love with.

I would return to the house with my books. The sky was gray some days, typical in the summer in Mexico, before it rains. I loved that gray bright light, walking down those white gray streets. It's not what one would expect from sunny Mexico, but Mexico City is in some respects a composition of grays. You might think it sounds grim, but it was like being in some fancy European town to me. With my books under my hand, I felt transported, connected to history. I was walking toward a future where I would be the next Siqueiros.

The "next Siqueiros," mind you, was the son of a bathroom salesman.

The entrance to our house was a storefront that my dad had made by retrofitting the garage. It was called Helguera y Compañía. My grandfather had created a small bathroom and kitchen supply business in Mexico City that prospered, and he had mentored my dad, his eldest son, to lead it. By the time my father took over and my grandfather passed away, the debts, union fights and other financial challenges led to the business's downfall. So when I was four years old, we moved to this smaller house in colonia Nápoles, where my father restarted as a new small business.

A row of toilets, sinks and medicine cabinets were lined up at the store's entrance so that clients could browse the merchandise for sale. Colorful, patterned tile samplers lined a back shelf, showing the products by various fabricators that were available. The space was a bit disorienting, as if, when walking into someone's house, what you expect to be the entryway or foyer is actually the bathroom. There is something odd about bathroom showrooms; it feels a bit embarrassing to be in this public space that's typically a place of privacy, as if you were expected to go to the bathroom in the plain view of strangers. Bathrooms are a place where we feel at ease, protected at our most vulnerable whether in the process of cleaning ourselves or easing our bodily needs. And yet, in the store, this room was the most public.

Strange juxtapositions would take place in the confrontation between the public and the private. My dad sold bidets – and in fact we had bidets installed all over the house. Prospective clients would sometimes not know what those objects were, and my father had an elegant way of describing them: "they are designed to aid in the process of making the seat bath more comfortable."

I could have never imagined that one day, I would discover a relationship between that toilet showroom and the Polyforum. That those olive green bidets and Interceramic tiles would one day be connected to that multi-angular concrete building with massive swollen muscular figures and violent perspectives endeavoring to transform the social order of the universe.

My small social order, the social order of a Mexican kid growing up in a middle-class neighborhood with American street names, in a house with a toilet showroom across from a stationery store and a carpenter, would nonetheless become part of my mindset as an artist.

Because you know what? There is a connection between those strangely named streets and art history, between toilets and museums. The language of art, when it becomes international and exported around the globe, names everything in the periphery. Everything gets subsumed in dominant terminology. Arizona street, where I grew up, is to the State of Arizona as Land art and process-based art were to my youthful strolls and initial learnings as an artist. Marcel Duchamp and his Urinal were already there, in my dad's garage in Colonia Nápoles, and I did not know it. Later, when I worked in art museums, I thought of those showrooms. I thought about display.

And I thought about those bidets.

June 3, 2020

A garden courtyard in Brooklyn.

Pablo

The days are gloomier and gloomier. There is no respite. It is becoming increasingly difficult to continue working in any productive way at this point. I feel most of us are trying to not get overcome by paralysis, anger, and sadness.

Today is my father's birthday. He would have turned 94 years old today. He was the eternal optimist and enjoyed simple pleasures. He was often moved to tears by pieces of music. He loved sunsets and lying on the grass—something that never appealed to me very much. A few weeks ago, one night, Estela proposed for us to go downstairs to the small yard in our complex to "stargaze". Now we go downstairs every night and lie on the grass to look at the stars. These have become very meaningful moments to me and have made me realize how I am connecting to my dad in the same way that Estela is connecting with me during these difficult days. She is 11, and as she runs around the garden at night, I think about how this, also, is a way by which she is saying goodbye to her childhood.

My mom used to tell the story of a distant relative—the cousin of the daughter of the sister of the uncle of the twice-removed cousin, perhaps—a child who, in the 1940s started losing his sight, until he could only distinguish distant lights. He spent the days next to a radio console of the family, which had a small red light that lit when the console was turned on. He spent hours with his eyes next to the red light, turning it on and off, on and off.

Yesterday I was at the park near my house. I sat on a park bench, looked out to the sun, and sought to think of myself in a different place. A luminous place without feelings. My eyes are closed, but I know this place exactly and recreate it in my mind, as in a dream

The street feels small. It is luminous, but one could almost feel that everything has been simplified. Maybe it is simplified because it is a dream, so the trees, the pavement, the houses, all have brighter colors and more uniform shapes, kind of if we were in a Sesame Street set. The street is active; people are walking around it. There is activity. There are children on the swings, their voices forming the typical, indecipherable medley that characterizes these places. It could be a Saturday morning, like all the Saturday mornings I always have loved. Or it could be the end of the day on Friday, when the weight of the week can finally be taken off the adult's shoulders and they go home, perhaps to have a drink. Or maybe it is Tuesday morning, when you see all these mothers who don't have to work, usually because they are affluent and don't have to worry all the time about money like me, carrying their toddlers, and cleaning after them, letting them crawl on the toddler area of the park.

It doesn't matter what day of the week it is. And it doesn't matter what my feelings are; they are completely irrelevant. What matters is that I am there, and the images I am seeing. I can see the park building, where the bathrooms are located—but in this dream I know there is something else in the building—something that has been there for hundreds of years, maybe thousands. A portal to another universe, to another reality that is incomprehensible to everyone but to me.

I am like that distant relative, losing my own eyesight, not literally, but in a much greater sense. I am turning that light on and off, repeatedly, trying to catch a signal perhaps. Trying to understand something about my life that I still cannot grasp.

Today is June 3, 2020. My father's birthday.

I need my father's optimism, his positive outlook, more than ever.

Second Aisle

Living room. There are four chairs with music on them. There is a blue rug and a table with many ashtrays on it.

Steinway appears in the middle of the space.

Steinway

Interestingly, the thing I remember the most about our family's living room in the house on Arizona Street is the cigarette smell, even though none of us who lived there were smokers. But whenever we had visitors they would often smoke, and the smoke would reach the second floor of the house where our bedrooms were. I was often hiding there, shy and unwilling to come downstairs to say hello. I was a shy kid, about 6 years old.

We did have ashtrays, lots of them, of every shape and form, mostly my grandfather's collection. Many of them were made of glass. As a child, I was fascinated with them.

We also had a fireplace, and I loved helping my parents start the fire. Every child loves starting a fire.

As kindling, we would use remnants of a huacal, which were wooden crates used for transporting toilets, and would roll pieces of a newspaper to get the fire started. It was hypnotizing to see the fire.

One time, for reasons that I can't remember, I decided to surreptitiously wrap the fancy glass ashtrays on the living room table in newspaper and throw them one by one in the fireplace, which we used from time to time. The popping sounds of the breaking glass alerted my mom that something odd was going on. When she confronted me, asking who had thrown the ashtrays into the fireplace, I replied: "I would rather not talk about it."

Perhaps at that time, instinctively, I was making an artwork. Throwing the containers of ashes into the fireplace so that they can become ashes themselves is a poignant, poetic action. Maybe I was trying to communicate something.

The second thing that the living room makes me think about is music. There was a mid-size Steinway piano where my sister practiced incessantly, obsessively, day and night. It might be strange for some to think of a household in Mexico where the only music heard was Bach, Mozart, Brahms, Debussy or Ravel. In the 1940s, my grandfather had decided that he will have his 4 sons each learn an instrument and play together. He hired two Hungarian musicians who had fled Europe during the war, Roth and Hartmann, to teach the children. My father, the older one, was the violinist. Together they formed the cuarteto Helguera. When I look at the living room I think of collaborative work, which is absolutely crucial for playing chamber music.

I was also one of 4 siblings, and was the youngest. My older sisters played the piano and the cello. My brother listened to Ravel, Debussy, Stravinsky. There was classical music coming out of the house from all directions, all day long. My sister the pianist would practice day and night on the baby grand Steinway, and our dog slept under it—the prime audience of all the Chopin Études and Nocturnes she practiced.

Like the odd American streets that surrounded our neighborhood, I only knew the Spanish version of the titles of the musical pieces that my family practiced or listened to. Tocata y Fuga, Preludio, fuga y variación, Pavana para una infanta difunta, valses nobles y sentimentales.

The third thing I remember when I think about the living room is the household objects.

There were a group of Murano glass birds, a set of gold painted blue wine glasses which I thought were extremely fancy when I was a child, a bronze bust of Beethoven and many other family heirlooms inherited from our grandparents and sometimes our great-grandparents. None of them had any significant monetary value, but the amount of stories and family history they contained made them treasures to us.

We also had a reproduction of the goddess Guanyin, which at the time we called "the Chinese Goddess."

Guanyin is a Buddhist deity of happiness, and is often depicted holding a lotus flower. Usually, large Guanyin figurines have a cavity in their bodies, and you can remove the goddess's hand to deposit a wish inside the figurine. We did this a lot throughout our childhood. We asked Guanyin to help us pass exams, to make our crushes reciprocate our love, or for happiness. The figure is still around, with all those secret wishes inside its body.

When my family emigrated to the United States, we brought a lot of those things with us. They became our only physical connection to our past in a country that seemed to be made of plastic, where the majority of things looked attractive and practical but had no artistic value—they were 99 cent objects. Those 99 cent objects were not real for me, perhaps because they felt disposable. In contrast, the objects that my mom had brought from Mexico were irreplaceable. One of them was a sío, a silver finger bowl, filled with warm water and lemon, used to wash your fingers while eating an artichoke—a remnant of a luxurious life that felt so remote at that time. Yet, on Sundays my father would sit on the dining room table and polish this and other silver objects using a white smelly silver cleaning detergent.

My mother would use a red liquid to polish the dining room table.

I do apologize, I'm not sure why these days I'm only thinking of containers and smells. Ashtrays, bowls, wine glasses, cíos, cigarette smell, silver polishing liquid smell, red wood polishing oil smell. Chinese goddesses as containers of wishes. But I guess one could argue that a life could be described exclusively through containers and smells we encountered along the way.

But the main point I want to make here is that sometimes we become the subjects of objects. It happens in silence, over the years. Especially when we love objects. We collect them because we become sentimentally attached to them, because they remind us of things we want to remember. But then, eventually, we become little more than the collection of objects around us. And then we develop a terrible fear, the fear that if all those objects disappeared one day, we could disappear ourselves. This can become the collector's curse.

Museums are containers of wishes, containers of ashes of ideals.

Which makes me think that I could make an argument that no one has ever made before: everything you need to know about art and museums, you can learn in a 19th century living room with a fireplace surrounded by family heirlooms, and from a toilet showroom.

Third Aisle

A museum office.
Pablo comes to center stage.

Pablo

I have sometimes wondered: if there is an afterlife, what makes us think that we would retain our memories after dying? It is always assumed that we become souls in heaven, connected to our past, watching over our loved ones on earth. But what if we simply became oblivious, memory-less souls? What if heavenly bliss was precisely the unburdening of our memories?

As a child I would sometimes visit my aunt Elena in her office. She ran the public programming of the Auditorio Julian Carrillo of Radio Universidad Autónoma de México. It was a small auditorium that I was very fond of, perhaps because of its comfortable orange seats (made in about 1980) but also because this was the place where I started my artistic education. Because it was a university cultural center, my aunt would have to organize events there constantly, but most of the time hardly anybody came to them. So my aunt would frantically call my mother to send me over as an audience member for whatever they were presenting that night.

My aunt did not have a big budget, but she needed to maintain an active schedule of activities, which made her resourceful. She had a knack for making contracts with the Swedish, the French or the American Embassies to present "ciclos de cine," or film series. This is how I watched, mostly in solitude, all of Ingmar Bergman's films, and a good portion of the masterpieces of the silent film era. Often it was only me and the projectionist in the auditorium. On other occasions I saw famous Mexican writers lecture and read poetry, and musicians interpret pieces by contemporary composers.

Of those experiences, the one that remains the strongest in my memory is the one of me and my aunt being the last ones in the orange auditorium at the end of the night, and she turning off the lights. Perhaps because of those early experiences, I often have the desire to be the last one to leave the auditorium after a program ends—to maybe try to feel the energy that lingered in the room.

These early moments would later connect with my museum career, which came about unexpectedly. I started working in museums back in 1991. I was a recent art school graduate, coming from performance. So ever since that time, organizing live events has been a natural activity for me. I enjoyed the rituals around it. Having an official ID hanging from my neck, working in the safe and spacious backstage, sitting in a quiet office.

Over the years I found myself doing a job for which there was no structured career path. The profession did not really have an official name. I was not a curator nor a conservator. Not exactly a museum educator, but rather: a public programmer, a ghostwriter of experiences.

(*Arizona enters*)

Arizona

The difference between me and my co-workers at the museum was clear. I was a practicing artist, while most of them were not. Or if they were, they weren't pursuing art professionally. But when they learned I was a practicing artist they would sometimes say, "yes, we all are artists." I don't intend to deny that there's creativity in every facet of life, but under that criteria lawyers, tax attorneys and politicians also are artists.

When I was first hired at one of those museums, the first few months were wonderful. I was told by my then supervisor,

Pablo

"Don't you feel like you have died and gone to heaven?"

Arizona

Indeed it was a well-paid job, in a beautiful, climate-controlled environment, working with the most knowledgeable people in the field. A privilege indeed.

I eventually noticed that there was an unspoken tradition of artists working within the institution. Edward Steichen, Phillip Johnson and Frank O'Hara, for example. In most cases, however, perhaps except Johnson, their roles as administrators, curators or educators superseded their contribution as artists—something that always worried me.

I worried about this because I sensed that the work of the curators, educators and administrators was primarily invisible, especially when it was good—like the invisible hand that guides the experience, but without determining it. Like a ghostwriter. I did not want to be invisible. I did not want to be merely a ghostwriter. But I then felt guilty, thinking that my desire to be recognized as an artist was egotistical.

I had the prevalent sense that I, an artist amidst the elite realm of modernism, would not last a single day. One of the things I realized was, first, that my role in this place was not seen as mattering a great deal—like Claudius, I was the idiot of the family, of the community of the power-hungry. Under a veneer of cordiality and civility, many of my colleagues were, in fact, in fierce competition to occupy the galleries with their curatorial vision. Unlike Claudius, however, I thankfully never became emperor. I never even wanted to be part of that internal hierarchy at all: I was a different species, and I knew that the day would come when I would leave that place and hopefully continue my life as an artist.

I'm not sure if it's the result of having a high regard for myself, or pretentiousness, or simply being an artist, but I ultimately resented submitting to that type of invisibility. It seemed humiliating. Self-regard, and perhaps a degree of vanity, do not let us want to be merely the context for great things to happen, but instead to be the context-maker.

(*Steinway enters*)

Steinway

The non-practitioner arts professional (that is, the person whose job is to support the presentation of art made by others) has a fascinating and mysterious psychology. Like the Beta individuals in Aldous Huxley's *Brave New World*, uniform in their mulberry-colored clothing, assisting the superior Alphas in their intellectual works, the non-artist art professional is ultimately an individual who implicitly accepts their secondary role. They perhaps think to themselves: we in this museum know that we are here for the art, and that without it we would be nothing. But we don't spend any time reflecting on that fact. In order to compensate for the sense of inferiority that this condition provides, this person finds validation in his or her expertise in the management of art, whether it's in the way it's preserved, presented or interpreted, as well as how promoting the museum can bring revenue through membership, ticket or store sales. There is an unspoken sense that the artist produces an important product, but that they're irrelevant when it comes to the logistics of making that work available to the masses. This is something I call "the art technician syndrome."

I *was* an art technician. Someone whose role was not a maker of art, but a creator of platforms for its distribution. As an art technician, I was too experienced to ultimately disregard the value of art—as it would amount to a disregard for my own expertise. Instead there is a treatment of the object in a pragmatic way, a clinical study of its features, potential and problems. To express passion for the object is uncommon, and might be seen as unprofessional.

One day another art technician, a colleague of mine, asked me in reference to the artists exhibited at our museum:

Arizona

"You don't really care about being an artist like them, do you?"

Pablo

"What are you talking about?" I said. "Of course I care."

Steinway

My colleague was confounded by my response—they looked at me like I was crazy, or stupid, or immature. I was clear that they had given up on being an artist long ago. For all that "everyone is an artist" rhetoric, they felt that a career as an artist was basically an egotistical endeavor.

I felt that my colleague had come directly from the nursery of *A Brave New World*, the place where Beta newborn babies were conditioned with a soft voice telling them how great it is to be a Beta, how you should never hope to bear the responsibilities of being an Alpha.

Pablo

One day, I finally left the museum. The exhilaration about finally having left for good gave way to another concern: I have left the museum, but will the museum ever leave my mind? I saw the best minds of my generation becoming consumed by that place afterward, immersed in terrible bitterness and resentment, having been completely defined by that atmosphere of self-importance. Their identity so dependent on it that without it they no longer knew who they were.

I remembered that phrase again: you died and went to heaven. I wanted to reverse that process. I didn't want that art technician heaven. I wanted to be reborn. But for it to happen, I needed to erase the memories. For that reason, it's unlikely I'll set foot in the museum ever again, as has happened with the other museums I've worked at in the past. The process requires forgetting, leaving that ghostwriting behind. Walking away.

Speaking of walking, I often saw myself walking through those galleries before the museum opened. There was always something thrilling about that solitude, of walking in front of priceless art works, all the result of complex life stories, many of which we will never fully know in depth, made by artists who largely didn't know that their works would be hanging on the public spaces of a major museum like that, one hundred years from when they were made.

Sometimes I would ask myself about the meaning of this container, and of my role in it.

This beautiful showroom of modernism, this public space that documented private creative expressions by some of the best minds known over the last hundred years, sometimes felt detached, clinical, academically remote. Its cleanliness felt oppressive.

And as much as I loved those art works and found them inspiring, within this highly designed, quasi-sacred architecture, I often saw myself, the art technician, as nothing but something closer to a museum label, a support mechanism. Like the household objects that take over our life, I became the subject of those museum objects. I was part of their collection. I was a forgotten wish, a handwritten crumbled piece of paper inside the darkness of the Chinese goddess.

Which brings me to the subject of words, those things that often fail us when we look at art.

When I left my museum life, as often happens when leaving a job, I took my personal items in cardboard boxes. They sat in my studio, unopened, for months.

I did not want to deal with them. As I said before, it was a chapter of my life that I wanted to leave behind. That I wanted to forget.

But then one day I finally had to open the boxes.

Inside were a number of notebooks, yellow pads, and journals that documented every conversation, every reflection I had as an art technician throughout those years. To-do lists. Reminders. Things I had heard someone say that were resonating in my brain. The phrases are unattributed, and they are not revealing of state secrets. They are like the phrases that a playwright jolts down on a notebook while overhearing people speaking on the subway. They are however an x-ray of the subconscious of an institution, of the words and ideas that circulate through it. As I read them, sitting in my studio, I started seeing them as the words and the feelings of another, or words without a particular owner, all of which come together to concoct a state of mind, like when we're falling asleep and the words that we heard throughout the day bounce around and resonate in our minds. Like in a carousel of conversations, they draw us deeper into slumber, like the voice in the neo-Pavlovian nursery carefully conditioning their babies to their assigned identity.

(*Pablo, Steinway and Arizona read from notecards*)

A+ artist A- artist

acting in a post-minimalist framework

always speaking the truth

Be critical of yourself

city talking to you (. . .) interpretation

designation of color as an artistic brand

different spiritual path

Don't underestimate the psychological impact

experience needs to be interpreted

Fluidity of boundaries

Follow through was not his forte

footnote panel

grandiosity is not the goal

information is not education

intellectual conversation

lobbying the elite

Marina / artist is present

misdirected tools to the wrong group

monetizing behavior

News from the Americas

no longer a space to linger

not about race

comments that represent how we want to be seen

Pretend play

Provisional Life

someone outside of art history

stepping into the light

tension between artificiality and truthfulness

The body as a political tool

the façade never cracks

the pendulum is swinging back

The Stopping of time

the thematic focus will be given by the containment of the structure

Tolerance of Ambiguity

too dependent on tourism

transitional societies

unauthored voice

utopian hardware

vigorously interpretive essays on objects

what gets lost when one becomes institutionalized?

what is best to do what can be done

whoever wants to become an artist should sign up

you try to win the "no one has heard of" prize

are we just shopping or do we have a collecting
strategy?

the majority of the time there's nothing

piece of reality

the social score

what is an exhibition

one thing can be many things at the same time

how to manage the expectations of the public

formal innovation / word and image

extremely successful even if beautiful

defining moments of conflict and contradiction

defamiliarize ourselves with space

check if this is happening

how long it takes to be disrupted

collective making leads to collective thinking

managing expectations

misinformation about images

aproximacion del principio de incertidumbre de un proyecto poético

the viewer is the context

voices of artists

Checkout

Pablo

Down in the subcellar of the museum, there is a room that no curator will allow you to see. It is a dark cave where some of the most tortured thinking takes place, where all the aesthetic debates, logistics, the clash of historical narratives and fire code compliances collide.

Arizona

The body remembers. The body reads. The body learns.

Steinway

They are sites for recovery, but also places where pain is neutralized.

Pablo

Like playing with little doll houses, the curators and exhibition designers place miniature objects one by one, like the hand of God, like Zeus from Mount Olympus placing figurines of mortals in the world as they face their fate. They look closely, they imagine the perfect gallery, visualizing how the world can be remade, or how it could it all be unraveled by simply placing that painting a few inches to the left.

Arizona

All those foreign names of streets must mean something. It must come from a desire to rub sophistication onto otherwise boring, uninteresting places.

Steinway

The glass ashtrays made crackling noises in the fire. They were announcing the process by which they would become ashes themselves. Which makes me wonder: don't we all become in a way the containers of the ashes of others, and then will become the ashes to be carried by those after us?

Arizona

Let's visualize what I am describing.

Steinway

Wrapping a beautiful thing on paper and throwing it to the fire.

Pablo

Carefully placing these objects in a palace of memory, one by one.

Arizona

Walking down the street feeling as if one is a world explorer,

Naming the roads in a foreign language: Nueva York, Pensilvania, Dakota, Indianápolis.

Steinway

Pavana para una infanta difunta, valses nobles y sentimentales,

Mamá la Oca, el rincón de los niños.

Arizona

Insurgentes Sur, Chicago, Patriotismo, San Pedro de los Pinos.

Steinway

Intermezzo número dos en sí bemol, opus ciento diecisiete.

Preludio, Fuga y Variación.

Preludio para la siesta de un fauno.

Juegos

Pablo

The art works, in that miniature, symbolic form, come to life. They speak to each other. The avatars of these art works whisper to the curators. Welcome to the model room, the place where all those art historical cataclysms are averted, where everything is measured, where no one will charge you admission or ask you not to stand too close to the work.

Steinway

They contain the music that was played in unison and the music that was dissonant.

Memories and desires are often written in small papers that are deposited inside secret slots.

Pablo

Here, in the model room, in this small version of the world, paths are created. But they are not pre-ordained nor completely open.

It is not that either you create your own path or all the paths have been walked. We live through desire paths, peripatetic learnings, dialogues, and the piling of the ashes of our experiences in small containers.

Arizona

As I walk down those streets, I ask myself whether all that walking was worth it.

All that dust that was carried, left behind.

Steinway

Memories and desires are like chamber music instruments. They all have different voices that propel us to action. We are the resulting composition.

I often think about all those wishes that never came true, those hopes that were left there, inside the Chinese goddess, forgotten.

And yet from those remnants, from those wishes, they must have served some purpose. Even if they were placebos that gave us strength to confront the future.

Pablo

We are often fond of transient places because they are devoid of memories and desires. Like our bodies, they are temporary containers of experiences. Which might be retained, or not, as we pass, and go, or not, to Heaven.

We read information as we walk.

The question I am left with is: am I the reader or the writer of the story? Or, since I am a ghost, are my memories real? Are they the inherited memories of someone else? How could I know?

Arizona

I pass a church, Iglesia Cristiana, calle Louisiana 163, colonia Nápoles. In it, I see a sign quoting from Isaiah 61:3:

Pablo

Aquaphor Baby Healing ointment is 9.99, buy one, get one 50% off.

Mommy's Bliss, baby constipation ease probiotic is $14.49. Vegan.

Arizona (*reciting*)

to bestow on them a crown of beauty

instead of ashes,

Pablo
Oral B complete floss is 4.99 with membership card.

Gum comfort slide flosser picks, Gentle, effective clean, is $4.99.

Arizona

the oil of joy

instead of mourning,

Pablo

Contour next, Blood Glucose Monitoring system, easy to use, is $21.99.

Aspercreme, Original soothe and relieve, with 10% Trolamine Salicylate, $7.79.

Sensodyne, complete protection for sensitive teeth and cavity prevention, $7.69.

Xlear Nasal Spray daily relief $12.99.

Arizona

and a garment of praise

instead of a spirit of despair.

Steinway (*reading from the few last notecards left*)

piece of reality

no longer a space to linger

define moments of conflict and contradiction

The Stopping of time

The façade never cracks.

(*lights fade to black*)

www.ingramcontent.com/pod-product-compliance
Lightning Source LLC
LaVergne TN
LVHW050943080826
845145LV00004B/1388

* 9 7 8 1 7 3 6 4 2 1 5 3 6 *